D0864802

English Cottages

Rose Cottage

Moor Farm Cottage

Old Barn House

The Oaks

Apple Cottage

# 55 COUNTRY
# CROSS STITCH CHARTS

# 55
# COUNTRY
# CROSS STITCH
# CHARTS

## Jane Greenoff

Have communion with few,
Be familiar with one,
Deal justly with all,
Speak evil of none.

*from a sampler by*
*Sarah Hubbard 1845*

**David & Charles**

To Bill, always

## THE INGLESTONE COLLECTION

The Inglestone Collection produces counted cross-stitch kits including some of the designs in this and previous books by Jane Greenoff. These are available from most good needlework shops or, in case of difficulty, by mail order.

To find out more about the above, please write (enclosing a stamped addressed envelope) to Jane Greenoff's Inglestone Collection, Yells Yard, Cirencester Road, Fairford, Gloucestershire GL7 4BS. Tel: 01285 712778.

Jane Greenoff founded the Guild in 1996 to promote the enjoyment of counted needlework of all kinds. For details of subscriptions, members facilities and further information contact: The Cross Stitch Guild, The Stable Courtyard, Longleat House, Warminster BA12 7NW.

**British Library Cataloguing-in-Publication Data**
Greenoff, Jane
    55 country cross stitch charts.
    I. Title
    746.44

    Hardback ISBN 0–7153–9952–7
    Paperback ISBN 0–7153–0606–5

Photography by Di Lewis
Charts by Ethan A. Danielson

Copyright Text, designs & charts © Jane Greenoff 1992, 1997
Photography © Di Lewis 1992, 1997

Reprinted 1992, 1993
First published in paperback in 1997

The right of Jane Greenoff to be identified as author of this work has been asserted by her in accordance with the Copyright, Designs and Patents Act 1988.

All rights reserved. No part of this publication may be reproduced, stored in a retrieval system, or transmitted, in any form or by any means, electronic, mechanical, photocopying, recording or otherwise, without the prior permission of David & Charles.

Typeset by ABM Typographics Ltd, Hull
and printed in England
by Butler & Tanner Ltd, Frome
for David & Charles
Brunel House   Newton Abbot   Devon

# Contents

# Introduction

The idea for this country chart book came quite unintentionally! After finishing my second cross stitch book I took time to enjoy our Cotswold cottage and the lovely countryside around us. However, living in the country and being a self-confessed cross stitch addict, I suppose the consequences were probably inevitable, as the countryside and the images it creates really lends itself to all forms of embroidery, but particularly to counted cross stitch – the greatest problem when the ideas came thick and fast was where to stop!

This book is intended for cross stitch enthusiasts everywhere, with pages of coloured charts all with a country theme that can be used for cross stitch on both evenweave fabrics and canvas. Many of the charts can be adapted for work on canvas using wool and/or stranded cottons; where appropriate, an exchange chart for Paterna wool has been included. Which canvas type is used has been left to personal choice and the needs of the end product. All that needs to be checked is the number of strands needed to cover the canvas effectively; you will find it helpful to work a small test area if you are not familiar with the yarn.

How to complete some of the more complicated projects is described in Useful Techniques (p115). If you need more detailed instructions about counted cross stitch, you will need to refer to my previous books or any of the other excellent cross stitch books published by David & Charles.

## THE CHARTS

All the charts in the book have been used in some form in the projects photographed, either as in individual items or as part of a larger project.

Each motif on the charts is numbered, as are the charts themselves. You will see from the photographs throughout the book that some of the designs have been used more than once, thus demonstrating the adaptability of charted needlework. This simple system of numbering the motifs and charts will help you find your way around the charts, and it makes it easy to select the motifs you need for the larger projects. For example, to stitch the tree sampler on p41 you will need border 13 on chart 2 (p13), garland motifs 74 and 75 on chart 36 (p78), the alphabet on chart 18 (p42), the tree motif on chart 19 (p43) and the apple motif, 103 (p112).

The charts are all in colour, and the colour key on the chart itself is noted in DMC shade numbers unless stated. This number refers to the shade used for the stitched model in the colour picture. You will find threads in alternative colours also listed in the text; these have been specially selected to suit each project and to blend with each other, so you may see more than one alternative shade for any colour. In a few cases no suitable alternatives are shown because this is just not possible!

# THE FABRICS

A number of different fabrics have been used in the worked examples in the photographs, all of which should be readily available in good needlework shops or possibly by mail order. Where the type of fabric is of particular importance to the completed project it will be mentioned at the beginning of the section, although a complete list of fabrics used can be found on p114. As already mentioned, you should feel free to experiment with your own ideas and any spare pieces of material you have carefully saved! When you select a piece of fabric for a particular design, check the thread count of your material and the stitch count of the design you have chosen. This is most important if the completed project has to fit a particular frame, card or trinket pot.

# THREADS

If you want to repeat the effect shown in the colour photographs you must use the colours and threads shown on the colour charts, which are also denoted by * in the text. The other lists of threads are provided for those who prefer to use other ranges of threads.

**DMC stranded cotton** is a six-ply mercerised thread which is usually divided, the most appropriate number of strands being used for the design and the fabric of your choice.

**German flower thread** is a single ply, unmercerised cotton thread which is used singly for cross stitch and gives an attractive matt finish to the work. It can be very effective to contrast the two types of yarn in one project. In some designs you may prefer to outline the cross stitch in one strand of stranded cotton rather than the flower thread, to give a more delicate finish.

**Paterna wool,** a pure virgin wool spun and dyed in England, has a beautiful rich lustre. It is a three-ply yarn and is very adaptable, and can be combined with stranded cotton to good effect.

**Designer silk** is space-dyed by hand and blended throughout the spectrum, so that the colour changes are delicate and subtle. Each length gradually changes colour, from a dark shade at one end to a lighter shade at the other, so the stitcher can work subtle colour changes without continuously changing threads. The yarn is sold in mixed skeins, often including more than one colour or shade. When working cross stitch with Designer Silk it is important that each cross stitch is worked individually rather than in two journeys.

# WASHING AND PRESSING
# CROSS STITCH

When a project is complete, check for missed stitches and loose ends. If necessary the design may be washed in hand-hot water with a soap-based product, rinsed well and dried naturally. To press cross stitch, cover the ironing board with a thick, soft white towel and press the needlework on the wrong side with a hot iron. NEVER press cross stitch on the right side as you will flatten all your endeavours!

**NB** Imperial measurements are used throughout, with metric equivalents in brackets.

# Borders

Many cross stitch designs use a stitched border to 'frame' the picture, although it depends both on personal choice and the type of project you are planning. These two pages of charts can be used on your own designs or combined with other charts in the book to make up some of the illustrated models.

The colour codes for these charts refer to the thread used for the border designs throughout the book.

## CHART 1:

### Pink Carnation (motif 1)

| Colour | *GFT | DMC | ANCHOR | PATERNA |
|---|---|---|---|---|
| Cherry | 2088 | 3350 | 0896 | 903 |
| Rose pink | 2068 | 335 | 038 | 905 |
| Sage green | 3001 | 320 | 0261 | 602 |
| Medium green | 2000 | 989 | 0241 | 613 |

### Corner A (motif 2)

| Colour | GFT | *DMC | ANCHOR | PATERNA |
|---|---|---|---|---|
| Green | 3902 | 937 | 0263 | 601 |

### Corner B (motif 3)

| Colour | GFT | *DMC | ANCHOR | PATERNA |
|---|---|---|---|---|
| Pale green | 2099 | 772 | 0259 | 614 |
| Medium green | 2001 | 988 | 0262 | 612 |
| Dark green | 3902 | 937 | 0263 | 601 |

### Red and Blue Borders (motifs 4, 5 and 6)

| Colour | GFT | *DMC | ANCHOR | PATERNA |
|---|---|---|---|---|
| Pink | 2041 | 3350 | 0896 | 903 |
| Blue | 3122 | 930 | 0851 | 511 |
| Green | 2001 | 988 | 0262 | 612 |

CHART 1
BORDERS

## CHART 2:

*Single colour borders* (motifs 7 and 8)

These simple borders can be stitched in any colour, in any yarn and are often useful around a simple design as shown on p41, little alphabet.

*Flower borders* (motifs 9 and 12)

These two pretty little designs are not seen stitched in the book, but could be used as an alternative to suggested borders.

*Traditional strawberries* (motif 10)

| COLOUR | GFT | *DMC | ANCHOR | PATERNA |
|---|---|---|---|---|
| Dark green | 3902 | 937 | 0263 | 600 |
| Light green | 3001 | 989 | 0261 | 602 |
| Honey | 2003 | 738 | 0372 | 405 |
| Purple | 2011 | 327 | 0872 | 321 |

*Pink and Blue Stars* (motif 11)

| COLOUR | GFT | *DMC | ANCHOR | PATERNA |
|---|---|---|---|---|
| Cornflower | 3403 | 340 | 0118 | 342 |
| Pale blue | 1022 | 341 | 0117 | 343 |
| Pink | 1002 | 335 | 038 | 904 |

*Blue carnation* (motif 13)

| COLOUR | GFT | *DMC | ANCHOR | PATERNA |
|---|---|---|---|---|
| Dark blue | 3722 | 930 | 0851 | 511 |
| Light blue | 1022 | 932 | 0850 | 513 |
| Dark green | 3902 | 501 | 0878 | 532 |
| Light green | 2099 | 503 | 0875 | 523 |

CHART 2
BORDERS

# Butterflies, Birds, Harvest and Hedgerow

Although wildlife is a little more difficult to work in cross stitch, the finished effect can be quite charming. The designs on the following pages have been made up as the butterfly and ladybird alphabet, James's country diary, the silk holder and the butterfly crystal pot as illustrated on p16.

CHART 3

## BUTTERFLIES

The butterfly is always a popular motif for both counted cross stitch and canvaswork. These pretty designs can be used on their own or combined with other designs as illustrated on p16. A butterfly has been stitched in stranded cottons for the lid on a crystal pot and made to the manufacturer's instructions. The same butterfly but different colourway is used as part of the butterfly and ladybird sampler. Small butterflies from this chart have been used on the country sampler on p37, but this time stitched in German flower thread.

| *DMC | ANCHOR | PATERNA |
|------|--------|---------|
| 798 | 0941 | 541 |
| 809 | 0129 | 545 |
| 321 | 019 | 951 |
| 758 | 0337 | 954 |
| 938 | 0381 | 430 |
| 712 | 0387 | 261 |
| 722 | 0323 | 803 |
| 327 | 0872 | 321 |
| 304 | 047 | 950 |
| 350 | 011 | 842 |
| 352 | 09 | 843 |
| 353 | 06 | 845 |
| 840 | 0393 | 462 |

| *GFT | DMC | ANCHOR | PATERNA |
|------|-----|--------|---------|
| 2068 | 335 | 038 | 942 |
| 2021 | 3326 | 026 | 945 |
| 1821 | 211 | 0342 | 322 |
| 3512 | 640 | 0393 | 462 |
| 2022 | 799 | 0850 | 513 |
| 3332 | 209 | 0109 | 303 |

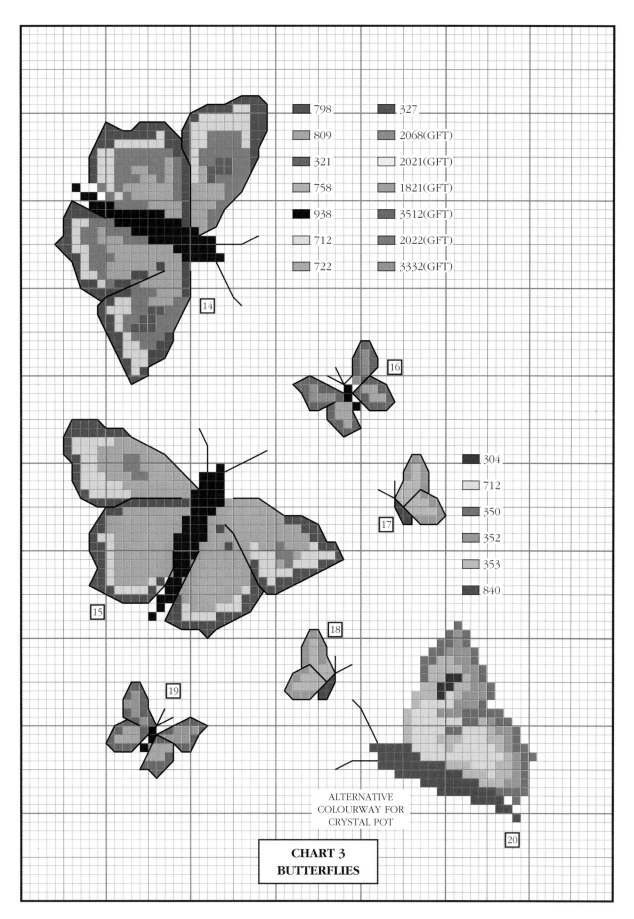

798 327
809 2068(GFT)
321 2021(GFT)
758 1821(GFT)
938 3512(GFT)
712 2022(GFT)
722 3332(GFT)

14

16

304
712
350
352
353
840

17

15

18

19

ALTERNATIVE
COLOURWAY FOR
CRYSTAL POT

20

**CHART 3**
**BUTTERFLIES**

CHART 4

# BIRDS AND ANIMALS

These charming bird and animal designs have been made up into a book cover for James's country diary. The same designs could be used to cover a purchased loose-leaf binder or scrapbook cover (see Useful Techniques, p115).

| *DMC | ANCHOR | PATERNA |
|------|--------|---------|
| 898  | 0381   | 460     |
| 3032 | 0392   | 462     |
| 304  | 047    | 950     |
| 989  | 0261   | 613     |
| 712  | 0387   | 445     |
| 561  | 0218   | 661     |
| 415  | 0398   | 212     |
| 317  | 0400   | 210     |

CHART 5

| *DMC | ANCHOR | PATERNA |
|------|--------|---------|
| 632  | 0379   | 472     |
| 3032 | 0393   | 463     |
| 301  | 0349   | 721     |
| 975  | 0355   | 402     |
| 437  | 0362   | 405     |
| 301 + 3032 | 0349 + 0393 | 721 + 463 |
| 3033 | 0388   | 454     |
| 317  | 0400   | 201     |
| 415 + 317 | 0398 + 0400 | 203 + 201 |
| 415  | 0398   | 203     |
| 561  | 0218   | 661     |
| 989  | 0261   | 613     |

LEFT:
*Butterfly and ladybird alphabet, James's country diary, silk holder and crystal pot*

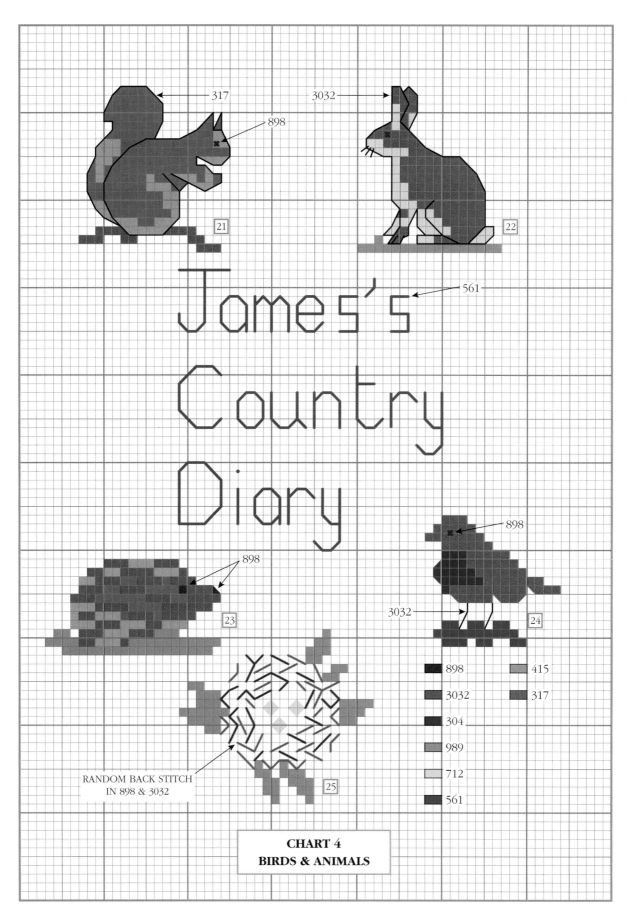

James's Country Diary

RANDOM BACK STITCH
IN 898 & 3032

| | |
|---|---|
| 898 | 415 |
| 3032 | 317 |
| 304 | |
| 989 | |
| 712 | |
| 561 | |

**CHART 4
BIRDS & ANIMALS**

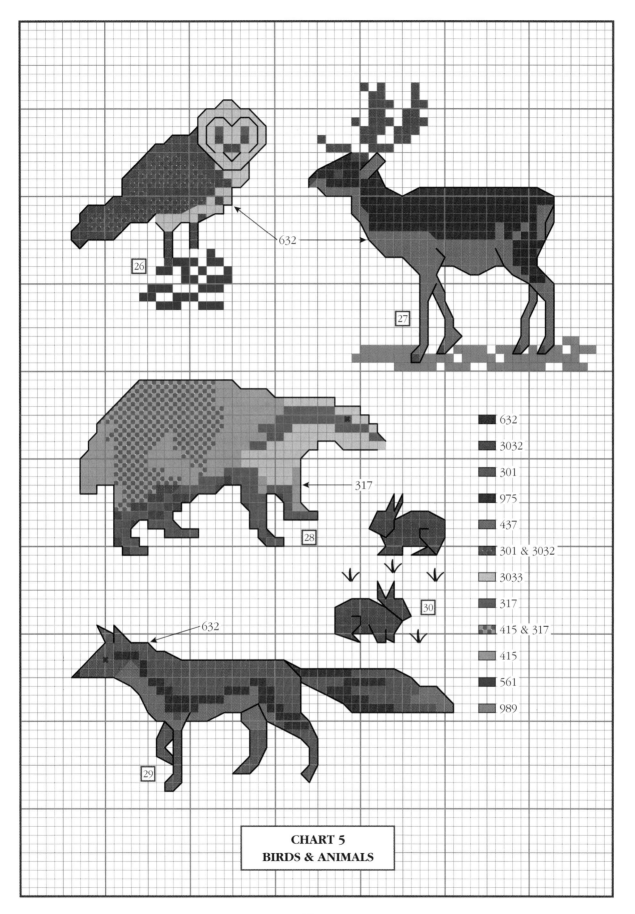

632

26

27

632

317

28

30

632

29

632
3032
301
975
437
301 & 3032
3033
317
415 & 317
415
561
989

**CHART 5**
**BIRDS & ANIMALS**

ANOTHER
COLOURWAY
USE 988 +
FOR LETTERS

CHART 6
BUTTERFLY AND LADYBIRD ALPHABET

# BUTTERFLY AND LADYBIRD ALPHABET

This pretty sampler is made of letters decorated with butterflies and ladybirds (chart 6, key on chart 7) and with the addition of butterflies from chart 3 (p15).

CHART 6 & 7

# ALPHABET & CORNFLOWER

| *DMC | ANCHOR | PATERNA |
|---|---|---|
| 320 | 0261 | 613 |
| 349 | 046 | 951 |
| 722 | 0323 | 854 |
| 3346 | 0267 | 621 |
| 327 | 0872 | 321 |
| 842 | 0378 | 472 |
| 712 | 0387 | 475 |
| (310) BLACK | 0403 | 220 |
| 792 | 0133 | 550 |
| 839 | 0936 | 471 |
| 809 | 0129 | 553 |

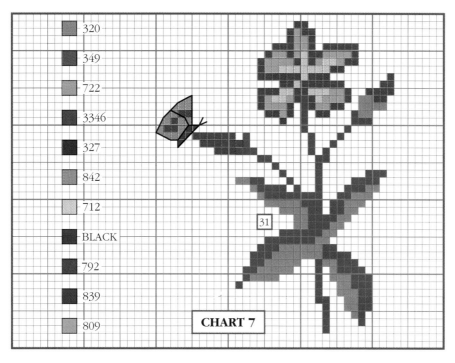

| | |
|---|---|
| 320 | |
| 349 | |
| 722 | |
| 3346 | |
| 327 | |
| 842 | |
| 712 | |
| BLACK | |
| 792 | |
| 839 | |
| 809 | |

CHART 7

CHART 8

# HARVEST AND HEDGEROW MOTIFS

The silk holder illustrated on p16 is stitched using the same basic letter as the butterfly alphabet but adding a poppy, cornflower, harvest mouse or dandelion to the letters. The whole alphabet could be stitched this way by tracing the letters from page 20 and adding the new motifs as shown.

| *DMC | ANCHOR | PATERNA |
|---|---|---|
| 834 | 0305 | 753 |
| 793 | 0123 | 544 |
| 936 | 0846 | 600 |
| 3347 | 0843 | 603 |
| 420 | 0375 | 434 |
| (310) BLACK | 0403 | 220 |
| 304 | 047 | 950 |
| WHITE | 01 | 260 |

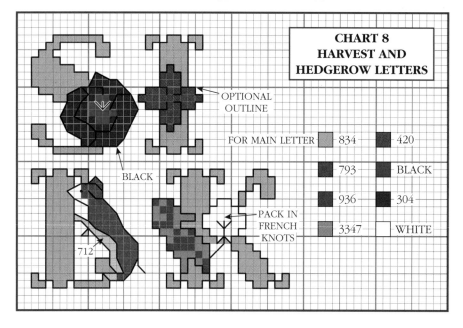

**CHART 8**
**HARVEST AND**
**HEDGEROW LETTERS**

OPTIONAL OUTLINE

BLACK

712

PACK IN FRENCH KNOTS

| FOR MAIN LETTER | 834 | | 420 |
|---|---|---|---|
| | 793 | | BLACK |
| | 936 | | 304 |
| | 3347 | | WHITE |

CHART 9

# HARVEST POSY

| *DMC | ANCHOR | PATERNA |
|---|---|---|
| 816 | 020 | 840 |
| 321 | 047 | 950 |
| 743 | 0298 | 726 |
| 437 | 0362 | 753 |
| 840 | 0379 | 472 |
| 3347 | 0843 | 603 |
| 936 | 0846 | 600 |
| (310) BLACK | 0403 | 220 |
| 793 | 0123 | 544 |
| 712 | 0387 | 327 |

**CHART 9
HARVEST POSY**

816
321
743
437
840
3347
936
BLACK
793
FRENCH KNOTS IN 712

840 →
840
840 →
BLACK →
437 →
FRENCH KNOTS IN 712
840 →
437
437 →

# Flowers and Alphabets

Flowers are probably the most popular subjects in counted needlework and can be used to decorate clothes, furnishings and all sorts of other objects.

The designs charted on pp27 and 29 have been stitched on a plain black waistcoat, an Afghan shawl and used in the purchased brush and comb set, all illustrated in the picture opposite. The waistcoat was cut out from a standard dress pattern and the flowers stitched before the waistcoat was completed. The brush and comb set was stitched on linen and made up as directed by the manufacturers. The shawl was stitched on Afghan fabric using alternate squares (see Fig 1) and then the edge frayed to a row of machine stitching.

As with many of the designs in this book, the outlines shown on the chart are not always necessary, so work the cross stitch first and then decide how much definition is required.

| A | | B | | E | |
|---|---|---|---|---|---|
| | D | | C | | F |
| C | | F | | A | |
| | B | | E | | D |
| E | | D | | C | |
| | F | | A | | B |

*Fig 1 Afghan Shawl*

RIGHT:
*Afghan shawl, brush and comb set and
embroidered waistcoat*

24

CHART 10

# SMALL FLOWERS AND POSIES

The small violets (motifs 34 and 35) are ideal designs for small projects like jewellery and trinket pots. The single red rosebud (motif 38) has been used as a corner motif on the rosebud cushion on pp68–9.

| *DMC | ANCHOR | PATERNA |
|------|--------|---------|
| 550 | 0102 | 310 |
| 988 | 0210 | 613 |
| 937 | 0263 | 610 |
| 224 | 0894 | 914 |
| 340 | 0118 | 561 |
| 809 | 0129 | 563 |
| 341 | 0117 | 564 |
| 727 | 0301 | 704 |
| 3350 | 0896 | 912 |
| 223 | 0895 | 913 |
| 470 | 0281 | 693 |
| 3685 | 0897 | 910 |
| 939 | 0152 | 570 |
| 552 | 0112 | 311 |
| 327 | 0872 | 312 |

**CHART 10**
**SMALL FLOWERS & POSIES**

| | 550 | | 340 | | 3350 | | 939 |
|---|---|---|---|---|---|---|---|
| | 988 | | 809 | | 223 | | 552 |
| | 937 | | 341 | | 470 | | 327 |
| | 224 | | 727 | | 3685 | | |

CHART 11

# LARGE FLOWERS AND POSIES

| *DMC | ANCHOR | PATERNA |
|---|---|---|
| 224 | 0894 | 914 |
| 939 | 0152 | 570 |
| 340 | 0118 | 561 |
| 352 | 09 | 843 |
| 3350 | 0896 | 912 |
| 758 | 0337 | 845 |
| 988 | 0262 | 612 |
| 3350 + 3685 | 0896 + 0897 | 912 + 910 |
| 223 | 0895 | 913 |
| 351 | 010 | 845 |
| 989 | 0261 | 612 |
| 937 | 0263 | 610 |
| 727 | 0301 | 714 |
| 891 | 035 | 843 |
| 341 | 0117 | 561 |
| 792 | 0123 | 560 |
| 712 | 0387 | 756 |

**B**

40

41

**F**

42

**E**

43

44

3350

**C**

**D**

45

**CHART 11**
**LARGE FLOWERS & POSIES**

| | 224 | | 988 | | 727 |
| --- | --- | --- | --- | --- | --- |
| | 939 | | 3350 | | 891 |
| | 340 | | 223 | | 341 |
| | 352 | | 351 | | 792 |
| | 712 | | 989 | | 3350 & 3685 |
| | 758 | | 937 | | |

**A**

46

# FLOWER ALPHABET

This charming, colourful alphabet has been stitched in two colourways to demonstrate how versatile it can be. It is charted over four pages in the green and pink colourway, with one letter shown in the dark blue version (chart 15B). These decorated letters are useful for adding initials to greetings cards or to a special gift.

The picture of the recipe folder and my daughter's name-plate (opposite) illustrates just how different this alphabet can look when alternative fabrics and threads are chosen. Both designs were stitched in stranded cotton, using two strands for the cross stitch. The outline illustrated on the chart is optional and could be worked in one strand of stranded cotton in a contrasting colour.

## CHARTS 12, 13, 14, 15A

| *DMC | ANCHOR | GFT |
|------|--------|------|
| 562  | 0216   | 1009 |
| 223  | 0895   | 1002 |
| 3350 | 0896   | 2088 |
| 727  | 0295   | 1049 |
| 712  | 0387   | 1001 |

## CHART 15B

| *DMC | ANCHOR | GFT |
|------|--------|------|
| 939  | 0152   | 3022 |
| 894  | 075    | 1002 |
| 602  | 063    | 2088 |
| 600  | 039    | 1105 |
| 727  | 0295   | 2084 |
| 712  | 0387   | 1001 |

RIGHT:
*Recipe folder and Louise name plate*

**CHART 12**
**FLOWER ALPHABET**

CHART 14
FLOWER ALPHABET

CHART 15A
FLOWER ALPHABET

562
223
3350
727
712

CHART 15B

939
894
602
600
727
712

# Samplers

## THE COUNTRY SAMPLER

This pretty traditional sampler was stitched using a single strand of German flower thread on linen. The picture (opposite) combines border no 1, the alphabet from chart 18 and butterflies, bird's nest and rabbits from charts 3, 4 and 5. The small amount of outline was added using one strand of stranded cotton in DMC shade 317. French knot roses and stones are added to the house and the outside of the pond after the cross stitch has been completed.

### CHARTS 16 and 17

| *GFT | DMC | ANCHOR |
|------|------|--------|
| 3112 | 937 | 0263 |
| 2081 | 340 | 0118 |
| 3822 | 932 | 0850 |
| 3001 | 320 | 0261 |
| 2088 | 3350 | 0896 |
| 2068 | 223 | 0895 |
| 1821 | 3608 | 970 |
| 1600 | 433 | 0357 |
| 1007 | 640 | 0393 |
| 2052 | 605 | 074 |
| 2096 | 351 | 010 |
| 2000 | 471 | 0265 |
| 3332 | 327 | 0872 |
| 1000 | 712 | 0387 |
| 1222 | 738 | 0372 |
| 2011 | 552 | 0112 |
| 3022 | BLACK | 0403 |
|  | 317 | 0400 |

RIGHT:
*The country sampler*

**CHART 16
DETAIL FROM COUNTRY SAMPLER**

ALL OUTLINE
IN DMC 317

1600

1600

1600

FRENCH KNOTS
IN 3112

FRENCH KNOTS
IN 2088

| | | | | | |
|---|---|---|---|---|---|
| 3112(GFT) | 3001(GFT) | 1821(GFT) | 2052(GFT) | 3322(GFT) | 2011(GFT) |
| 2081(GFT) | 2088(GFT) | 1600(GFT) | 2096(GFT) | 1000(GFT) | 3022(GFT) |
| 3822(GFT) | 2068(GFT) | 1007(GFT) | 2000(GFT) | 1222(GFT) | |

**CHART 17
DETAIL FROM COUNTRY SAMPLER**

1600

3822

1600

FRENCH KNOTS
IN 3112 & 1007

FRENCH KNOTS
IN 2088

# LITTLE ALPHABET AND TREE SAMPLER

The alphabet included in the tree sampler and seen illustrated on p41 as a sampler in its own right was taken from a design stitched in 1850. The tree sampler is an adaption of the theme of Adam and Eve often used by Victorian needlewomen. It uses border no 13 (p13), baskets of fruit from chart 29 (p62), the apple motif from chart 55 (p112), and the garlands from chart 36 on p78.

## CHART 18

| *DMC | ANCHOR | PATERNA |
|------|--------|---------|
| 930  | 0851   | 512     |
| 420  | 0375   | 441     |
| 738  | 0372   | 443     |
| 932  | 0850   | 513     |
| 436  | 0373   | 442     |

## CHART 19

| *DMC | ANCHOR | PATERNA |
|------|--------|---------|
| 433  | 0357   | 471     |
| 502  | 0876   | D546    |
| 3350 | 0896   | 901     |
| 501  | 0878   | D556    |
| 317  | 0400   | 210     |
| 727  | 0295   | 727     |
| 632  | 0379   | 472     |
| 898  | 0381   | 470     |
| 223  | 0895   | 904     |
| 945  | 0311   | 886     |
| 501  | 0878   | D516    |

RIGHT:
*The tree sampler and the little alphabet*

CHART 18
TRADITIONAL ALPHABET

**CHART 19**
**DETAIL FROM THE TREE SAMPLER**

433
502
3350
501
317
727
632
898
223
945

FRENCH
KNOTS

317

47

**CHART 20**
**THE VILLAGE SHOP**

| | |
|---|---|
| | 317 |
| | 340 |
| | 3032 & 415 |
| | 989 |
| | 937 |
| | PINK BEADS |
| | 725 |
| | 772 |
| | 436 |
| | 739 |
| | 738 |
| | 3033 |
| | 223 |
| | 224 |

317

ALGERIAN
EYE
340

48

317

317

3032

GREEN BEADS
937    772   FRENCH KNOTS    937

49

# The English Village

The picture illustrated on pp50–1 is a lovely design, putting together cottages, the church, the village pub and the shop, and even the village stocks, all surrounded by border no 10 on chart 2, p13. They are stitched in stranded cottons, and a few glass beads are used for added interest. The cross stitch is worked using two strands of stranded cotton, the outline in one strand of dark grey and the beads attached with a half cross stitch and one strand of matching thread. The Algerian eye is stitched using two strands of stranded cotton (see Fig 2 on p49) and can be seen in the illustration on pp50–1.

## THE VILLAGE SHOP

### CHART 20

| *DMC | ANCHOR | PATERNA |
|---|---|---|
| 340 | 0118 | 343 |
| 3032 + 415 | 0392 + 0398 | 463 + 203 |
| 989 | 0261 | 613 |
| 937 | 0263 | 610 |
| 725 | 0306 | 703 |
| 772 | 0259 | 614 |
| 436 | 0373 | 752 |
| 739 | 0361 | 755 |
| 738 | 0372 | 754 |
| 3033 | 0388 | 645 |
| 223 | 0895 | 913 |
| 224 | 0894 | 914 |
| 317 | 0400 | 200 |

## THE VILLAGE CHURCH

### CHART 21

| *DMC | ANCHOR | PATERNA |
|---|---|---|
| 937 | 0263 | 610 |
| 304 | 047 | 950 |
| 772 | 0259 | 695 |
| 834 | 0874 | 753 |
| 640 | 0393 | 462 |
| 3032 | 0392 | 463 |
| 3033 | 0388 | 465 |
| 415 + 317 | 0398 + 0400 | 203 + 200 |
| 436 | 0373 | 442 |
| 437 + 738 | 0362 + 0372 | 445 + 444 |
| 738 | 0372 | 444 |
| 898 | 0381 | 471 |
| 989 | 0261 | 613 |
| 317 | 0400 | 200 |

CHART 21
THE VILLAGE CHURCH

| | | |
|---|---|---|
| 937 | 834 | 3033 |
| 304 | 640 | 415 & 317 |
| 772 | 3032 | 436 |

| | | |
|---|---|---|
| 437 & 738 | 989 | |
| 738 | 317 | |
| 898 | | |

CHART 22
THE VILLAGE PUB

317

898

3032

ALGERIAN
EYE
340

340

937

317

51

| | 989 | | 415 | | 975 | | 738 |
| | 834 | | 340 | | 772 | | 436 |
| | 224 | | 327 | | 937 | | 640 |
| | 898 | | 3032 | | 304 | | 317 |

**CHART 23**
**COTSWOLD HOUSE, BARN AND STOCKS**

898

52

PINK
BEADS

898

53

898

898

937

54

| | |
|---|---|
| 3032 | |
| 640 | |
| 224 | |
| 223 | |
| 937 | 436 |
| 989 | PINK BEADS |
| 772 | 3032 & 415 |
| 898 | 738 |

48

# THE VILLAGE PUB, COTSWOLD HOUSE, BARN AND STOCKS

This pretty pub is stitched in a soft shade of pink rather like the plastered buildings that are common in some rural areas. The pond in the foreground is decorated in small beads to represent water plants; the rushes around the edge could be worked in cross stitch, French knots or by adding beads.

*Fig 2 Algerian eye (see chart 22)*

The technique of mixing the colours together to create a mottled effect is well illustrated here. In the roof of the Cotswold house it is particularly effective.

## CHARTS 22 and 23

| *DMC | ANCHOR | PATERNA |
|------|--------|---------|
| 989 | 0261 | 612 |
| 834 | 0874 | 753 |
| 224 | 0894 | 932 |
| 898 | 0381 | 470 |
| 415 | 0398 | 202 |
| 340· | 0118 | 343 |
| 327 | 0872 | 321 |
| 3032 | 0392 | 463 |
| 975 | 0355 | 402 |
| 772 | 0259 | 614 |
| 937 | 0263 | 611 |
| 304 | 047 | 970 |
| 738 | 0372 | 444 |
| 436 | 0373 | 443 |
| 640 | 0393 | 462 |
| 317 | 0400 | 210 |
| 223 | 0895 | 933 |

PAGES 50-1
*The English village sampler and tree picture*

# The Country Kitchen

## BREAD ROLLS AND HARVEST MOTIF

One of the most evocative images of living in the country is probably the farmhouse kitchen, complete with Aga and a scrubbed pine table covered with homemade preserves, dandelion wine and – best of all – crusty homebaked bread.

The bread bag as illustrated in the glorious picture on pp58–9 was actually inspired by a visit to Germany where bread is collected in purchased or homemade 'Brot' bags and the bag is simply washed in the washing machine as necessary. The bread roll cover pictured uses some of the bread motifs on one corner, a theme which could be extended to other things such as napkins.

### CHART 24

| *DMC | ANCHOR |
|------|--------|
| 898 | 0381 |
| 436 | 0373 |
| 725 | 0306 |
| 738 | 0372 |
| 304 | 047 |
| 420 | 0375 |
| 309 | 042 |
| 930 | 0851 |
| BLACK | 0403 |

## MAKING BAGS

All the bags illustrated in this book are made up in basically the same way. When the embroidery is completed, the design is pressed on the wrong side. Then place the right sides of the material together and stitch the edges by hand or machine (see Fig 3). The bread bag is lined with washable polyester and cotton fabric and includes a channel for the drawstring.

RIGHT SIDE

STITCHING LINE

CHANNEL FOR RIBBON

RIBBON

*Fig 3 Making the bread bag*

# CHART 24
## BREAD ROLLS AND HARVEST MOTIF

55

420

56

57

NOIR (Black)

420

420

58

| | | | | |
|---|---|---|---|---|
| 898 | 725 | 304 | 309 | NOIR (Black) |
| 436 | 738 | 420 | 930 | |

# CONDIMENTS

On this chart, familiar kitchen images have been used to make simple projects to decorate a shelf or even as part of a hamper intended as a gift. Any or all of these motifs could be combined to make up a kitchen sampler with great effect. Motifs nos 60 and 61 have been made up into bags for kitchen produce, and the blue cooking pot has been included in the oven mitt as seen illustrated on pp58–9.

All the designs on this chart were stitched in stranded cotton, using two strands for the cross stitch and one strand for the outlining.

## CHART 25

| *DMC | ANCHOR | *DMC | ANCHOR |
|------|--------|------|--------|
| 420 | 0375 | 3033 | 0388 |
| 738 | 0372 | 640 | 0393 |
| 436 | 0373 | 340 | 0118 |
| 930 | 0851 | 341 | 0117 |
| WHITE | 01 | 797 | 0133 |

## CHART 26

This simple chart gives the lettering for projects such as the magnetic fridge noteboard (p65) and the message board included in assorted projects (pp8–9). The message board (which comes complete with manufacturer's making up instructions) is stitched on aida in stranded cottons using borders 4, 5 and 6 from p11. It has the days of the week and a place to note 'things to do'.

# WINE BAG AND COFFEE MUG

The simple wine bag as illustrated on pp58–9 has been made up as a drawstring bag, but it could easily be adapted by adding a pair of handles and be used to carry the bottle of wine to a party! The super coffee mug is designed specially for cross stitch, and comes complete with a scrubbable plastic aida fabric.

All these designs were stitched in stranded cottons, using two strands for the cross stitch and one strand for the outline. The grapes on the coffee mug were stitched using the purple colourway, but using the small grape motif (no 63). The apple apron is a purchased linen apron with the cross stitched apple motif from chart 55 (p112) in three strands of stranded cotton.

## CHART 27

| DMC | ANCHOR | GFT |
|-----|--------|-----|
| 937 | 0263 | 3702 |
| 327 | 0872 | 2011 |
| 472 | 0278 | 2099 |
| 554 | 0109 | 2011 |
| 471 | 0279 | 3732 |
| 611 | 0832 | 5312 |

CHART 25
CONDIMENTS

Black Pepper

Coffee Beans

59

60

930

930

Sea Salt 930

61

640

420  640

738  340

436  341

930  797

3033  BLANC (White)

62

55

CHART 26
LETTERING CHART

Sun      Thur

Mon      Fri

Tue      Sat

Wed      Things to do

Forget-me-not

Jan      June      Nov

Feb      July      Dec

March    August

April    Sept

May      Oct

CHART 27
WINE BAG & COFFEE MUG CHART

937

63

937

327

937
327
472
554
471
611

64

*The bread bag, wine bag, coffee mug,*
*bread roll cover, oven glove, apple apron,*
*and linen bags for coffee beans, sea salt*
*and black pepper*

**CHART 28    FRENCH DRESSER**

| | 335 | | 739 | | 988 | | 436 | | 898 |
|---|---|---|---|---|---|---|---|---|---|
| | 340 | | 470 | | 420 | | 738 | | 712 |

# FRENCH DRESSER

A French dresser with a full display of china is a popular image from the farm-house kitchen, possibly as popular as the Aga. This simple design has been made up as a lovely card which could very well be framed.

The stitched version varies from the chart slightly in order to ensure the correct balance in the purchased card. Again, this motif would be ideal as part of a design for a kitchen sampler.

### CHART 28

| *DMC | ANCHOR |
|---|---|
| 335 | 041 |
| 340 | 0118 |
| 739 | 0366 |
| 470 | 0281 |
| 988 | 0262 |
| 420 | 0375 |
| 436 | 0373 |
| 738 | 0372 |
| 898 | 0381 |
| 712 | 0387 |

CHART 29
BASKETS OF FRUIT

898

66

501
3350
939
503
327
632
898

67

632
738
562
3350
966
223
224

68

3685
966
562
3350
224
327
433
436
738

**CHART 30
BASKETS OF FRUIT**

# BASKETS OF FRUIT

These lovely designs originated from Germany in the 1930s, yet they still look as modern and as fresh today. The colour picture on p65 shows two of the baskets (motifs 70 and 71) made up as small recipe holders, also preserve labels which use motif 69, and a magnetic fridge noteboard using motif 68. Motif 66 is used as part of the tree sampler design illustrated on p41. The clock is designed using motif 71 surrounded with random apples in matching colours, then made up to the manufacturer's instructions.

## CHART 29

| *DMC | ANCHOR | PATERNA |
|------|--------|---------|
| 501 | 0878 | 521 |
| 3350 | 0896 | 902 |
| 939 | 0152 | 570 |
| 503 | 0875 | 522 |
| 327 | 0872 | 321 |
| 632 | 0379 | 472 |
| 898 | 0381 | 430 |
| 966 | 0214 | 664 |
| 223 | 0895 | 905 |
| 224 | 0894 | 904 |
| 3685 | 0897 | 901 |
| 562 | 0216 | 662 |
| 433 | 0357 | 432 |
| 436 | 0373 | 435 |
| 738 | 0372 | 436 |

## CHART 30

| *DMC | ANCHOR | PATERNA |
|------|--------|---------|
| 300 | 0357 | 402 |
| 320 | 0261 | 613 |
| 309 | 042 | 941 |
| 352 | 09 | 863 |
| 743 | 0301 | 704 |
| 721 | 0324 | 802 |
| 722 | 0323 | 803 |
| 945 | 06 | 865 |
| 939 | 0152 | 570 |
| 937 | 0263 | 611 |
| 989 | 0262 | 612 |
| 3350 | 0896 | 902 |
| 931 | 0921 | 562 |
| 327 | 0872 | 321 |
| 352 + 945 | 09 + 06 | 863 + 865 |

RIGHT:
*Baskets of fruit, recipe holders and pictures, preserve labels, magnetic fridge noteboard and basket of fruit clock*

# Garlands and Cushions

## CHRISTMAS ROSE CUSHION

This gorgeous rose garland was inspired by a painting seen in Germany. The design is stitched on linen in stranded cottons, using two strands for the cross stitch and one for the outlining; the worked piece was then made into this lovely cushion, a fitting partner to the rosebud cushion – both are illustrated overleaf. The Christmas rose seen on each corner of the cushion in the colour picture is the single rose on the chart, reversed to fit the panel of the cushion.

The garland was also stitched on aida with the added ribbons as seen in chart 56 (motif 109) and set in the tray illustrated in the pictures on pp8–9 and pp68–9.

### CHART 31

| *DMC | ANCHOR | PATERNA |
|------|--------|---------|
| 937 | 0263 | 611 |
| 502 | 0876 | 662 |
| 562 | 0216 | 621 |
| 472 | 0278 | 671 |
| 727 | 0301 | 704 |
| ECRU | 0388 | 755 |
| 415 | 0398 | 202 |
| 712 | 0387 | 655 |
| 772 | 0259 | 614 |
| 792 | 0123 | 560 |
| 340 | 0118 | 562 |
| 471 | 0279 | 673 |
| 680 | 0901 | 732 |
| 725 | 0306 | 726 |
| 3350 | 0896 | 902 |
| 3685 | 0897 | 901 |
| 936 | 0846 | 601 |
| 224 | 0894 | 904 |
| 501 | 0878 | 661 |

PAGES 68-9
*Christmas rose cushion and round tray,*
*rosebud cushion, and wooden trinket box*

66

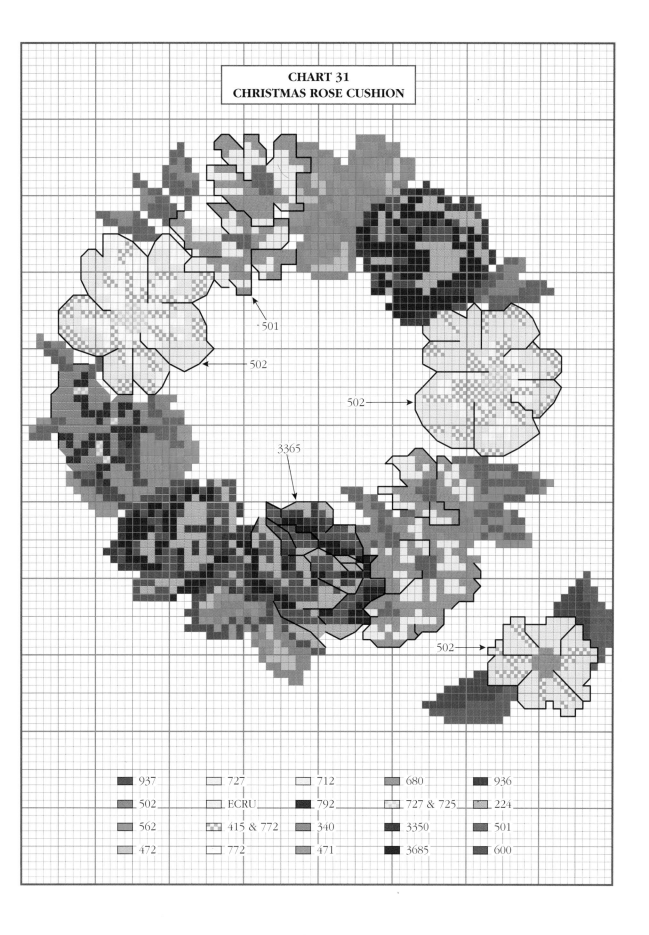

CHART 31
CHRISTMAS ROSE CUSHION

501

502

502

3365

502

| | 937 | | 727 | | 712 | | 680 | | 936 |
| | 502 | | ECRU | | 792 | | 727 & 725 | | 224 |
| | 562 | | 415 & 772 | | 340 | | 3350 | | 501 |
| | 472 | | 772 | | 471 | | 3685 | | 600 |

# ROSEBUD CUSHION

This Victorian garland was discovered on an old footstool, probably based on a Berlin chart. Here, it has been stitched on linen in stranded cottons, using two strands for the cross stitch and one for the outline.

This design and the Christmas rose on p67 have been made into cushions to prove just how effective cross stitch can be (see suppliers on p119). The rosebud design was also stitched in stranded cottons on canvas with a dark blue background supplied by Paterna. Once completed, the canvas was fitted into the top of the wooden trinket pot as seen in the pictures on pp8–9 and pp68–9.

### CHART 32

| *DMC | ANCHOR | PATERNA |
|------|--------|---------|
| 727  | 0301   | 704     |
| 680  | 0901   | 733     |
| 834  | 0874   | 663     |
| 3685 | 0897   | 900     |
| 223  | 0895   | 903     |
| 224  | 0894   | 904     |
| 433  | 0357   | 730     |
| 937  | 0263   | 601     |
| 470  | 0261   | 613     |
| 320  | 0262   | 612     |
| 939  | 0152   | 570     |
| 341  | 0117   | 562     |
| 792  | 0123   | 551     |

**CHART 32
ROSEBUD CUSHION**

| | | | | | | | | | |
|---|---|---|---|---|---|---|---|---|---|
| 727 | | 3685 | | 433 | | 320 | | 341 | |
| 680 | | 223 | | 937 | | 939 | | 792 | |
| 834 | | 224 | | 470 | | | | | |

# FLOWERS FOR PINCUSHIONS

These two simple motifs have been stitched in stranded cotton and made into pincushions as illustrated opposite. The single rose motif no 72 was combined with the heart-shaped garland on chart 36, motif no 77, adding a simple lattice-work effect with backstitch. If you are making these designs to fit purchased wooden bases, always check the design size with your fabric choice. Once the design is finished, make up as below.

## CHART 33

| *DMC | ANCHOR | PATERNA |
|---|---|---|
| 224 | 0894 | 906 |
| 3350 | 0896 | 902 |
| 223 | 0895 | 903 |
| 937 | 0263 | 611 |
| 3326 | 075 | 944 |
| 3687 | 069 | 904 |
| 761 | 031 | 945 |
| 989 | 0262 | 613 |

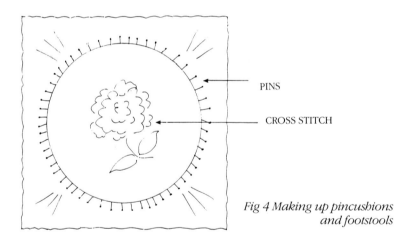

PINS

CROSS STITCH

*Fig 4 Making up pincushions and footstools*

# MAKING UP PINCUSHIONS AND FOOTSTOOLS

The footstool, pincushions and the wooden trinket box are all made up as follows: press the needlework on the wrong side with a warm iron and set aside. Undo the screw or screws on the bottom of the purchased wooden base and keep in a safe place. Mark the centre of the foam pad with a pin and do the same to the embroidery. Match the two points and, smoothing out the material as you go, pin the material to the bottom edge of the pad (see Fig 4). When you have pinned all the way round, check that there are no folds or puckers to be seen and that the design is in the right place, then lace in position as illustrated in Fig 7, p116. Replace the wooden base and screw in position.

RIGHT:
*Footstool and two wooden pincushions*

# FOOTSTOOL

The design is stitched in German flower thread and DMC stranded cottons and worked on unbleached linen, and then made into the lovely footstool as illustrated on p73. If preferred, the design could be stitched using wool on canvas. Where possible the colour key lists alternatives, though some of the shades have no equivalent.

## CHARTS 34 and 35

| *DMC | *GFT | ANCHOR | PATERNA |
|------|------|--------|---------|
| 550 | 1005 | 0102 | 311 |
| 939 | 3022 | 0152 | 570 |
| 902 | 3114 | 045 | 900 |
| 3685 | 2041 | 0897 | 901 |
| 335 | | 041 | 904 |
| 601 | 2073 | 078 | 961 |
| 352 | 3311 | 09 | 844 |
| 729 | 2082 | 0891 | 733 |
| 725 | 2084 | 0306 | 726 |
| 738 | 2003 | 0372 | 754 |
| 712 | 1001 | 0387 | 755 |
| 745 | 2061 | 0300 | 727 |
| 420 | 3302 | 0375 | 752 |
| 832 | | 0907 | 742 |
| 834 | | 0874 | 743 |
| 368 | 2000 | 0214 | 664 |
| 500 | 3702 | 0224 | 600 |
| 502 | 3902 | 0876 | 602 |
| 470 | 3212 | 0267 | 692 |
| 369 | 2001 | 0265 | 612 |
| 3348 | 2099 | 0260 | 614 |
| 677 | | 0305 | 745 |
| 833 | | 0907 | 753 |
| 562 | 3001 | 0216 | 662 |
| 783 | 1932 | 0307 | 713 |
| 327 | | 0872 | 321 |
| 3041 | 3432 | 0109 | 322 |
| 552 | 2011 | 0112 | 311 |

224
3350
223
937

3350

937

72

3326
937
3687
761
989

73

**CHART 33**
**FLOWERS FOR PINCUSHIONS**

CHART 34
FOOTSTOOL

550
939
3114 (GFT)
2041 (GFT)
335
601
3311 (GFT)
2082 (GFT)
725
738
712
2061 (GFT)
420
832
834
3702 (GFT)
3902 (GFT)
3212 (GFT)
2001 (GFT)
2099 (GFT)
368

601

CHART 35
FOOTSTOOL

601

420

677
833
3001 (GFT)
725
1932 (GFT)
327
3432 (GFT)
2011 (GFT)

1932

1932

CHART 36
GARLANDS

74

75

937

76

3350

327    727    3350
502    501    945

937
350
352

77

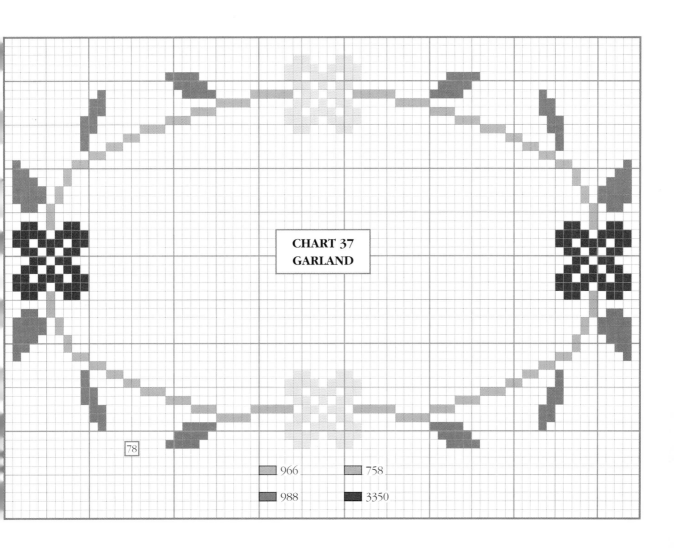

**CHART 37
GARLAND**

| | 966 | | 758 |
| --- | --- | --- | --- |
| | 988 | | 3350 |

78

# GARLANDS

These simple garland shapes make a useful addition to any project, for example to a sampler when embellishing initials or dates. Motifs 74 and 75 were used on the tree sampler on p41. The plain heart shape (no 77) was combined with the rose (chart 33, no 72) to complete the pincushion on p73. The large garland on chart 37 was used for the lovely 'new home' card – Winterfold Farm – illustrated on pp104–5.

| CHART 36 | | CHART 37 | |
| --- | --- | --- | --- |
| *DMC | ANCHOR | *DMC | ANCHOR |
| 327 | 0872 | 966 | 0214 |
| 502 | 0876 | 988 | 0262 |
| 727 | 0295 | 758 | 0337 |
| 501 | 0878 | 3350 | 0896 |
| 3350 | 0896 | | |
| 945 | 0311 | | |
| 937 | 0263 | | |
| 350 | 0334 | | |
| 352 | 09 | | |

79

# Seasons through the Archway

The archway designs depicting the four seasons – spring, summer, autumn and winter – are illustrated opposite. The following charts give the basic archway design, and you can add the seasonal detail from the chart as you prefer. The archway designs, and 'Rosegarth' which is illustrated on p86, are all stitched partly in 'Designer Silks' and partly in DMC and therefore involve a slightly different stitching technique.

Always work each cross individually rather than in two journeys. If you are unable to obtain Designer Silks, any sort of shaded thread would produce a similar effect using the technique as above, otherwise stranded cottons could be adapted as follows: group together different shades of one colour (eg greens or pinks) and pick them at random within the suggested colour range on the chart – thus, pick from the pinks for the flowers and allow the design to grow spontaneously.

## CHARTS 38 and 39

| *DMC | ANCHOR | *DMC | ANCHOR |
|------|--------|------|--------|
| 975 | 0355 | 738 | 0372 |
| 304 | 047 | 561 | 0218 |
| 898 | 0381 | 937 | 0263 |
| 640 | 0393 | 433 | 0357 |

## FOUR SEASONS BELL PULL

The bell pull described here is stitched on a linen band, but it could equally well be stitched on any evenweave material. If a band is used the stitch count must be checked carefully: as you will see from the illustration opposite, the garlands fit the band perfectly!

## CHART 40 and 41

| *DMC | ANCHOR | *DMC | ANCHOR |
|------|--------|------|--------|
| 834 | 0874 | 936 | 0846 |
| 727 | 0295 | 712 | 0387 |
| 743 | 0298 | 3350 | 0896 |
| 722 | 323 | 335 | 041 |
| 554 | 097 | 898 | 0381 |
| 327 | 0872 | 433 | 0357 |
| BLACK | 0403 | 304 | 047 |
| 605 | 074 | WHITE | 01 |
| 3364 | 0260 | 977 | 0313 |
| 772 | 0259 | | |

**CHART 38
SEASONS THROUGH THE ARCHWAY**

898

937

937

640

433

433

937

937

Spring

| | | |
|---|---|---|
| ■ D/S 611 | ■ D/S 607 | ■ 433 |
| ■ D/S 605 | ■ D/S 708 | ■ 304 |
| □ D/S 110(LIGHT) | ■ D/S 608(LIGHT) | ■ 898 |
| ■ D/S 110(DARK) | ■ D/S 608(DARK) | ■ 640 |

**CHART 39**
**SEASONS**

317

898

898

937

79 Summer

898

937

937

80 Winter

975

898

640

937

81 Autumn

| | | | | | |
|---|---|---|---|---|---|
| D/S 606(LIGHT) | 898 | 738 | D/S 302 | 561 | 937 |
| D/S 606(DARK) | D/S 617 | 304 | D/S 305 | D/S 313 | |

83

327 722 327

722

722

82

BLACK

3346

327

722

327

327

722

31
stiches

3350

554

335

335

327

335

327

3350

335

83

722

335

722

3350

722

722

834
727
743
722
554
327
BLACK
605
3364
772
936
712
3350
335
722 & 727

**CHART 40**
**BELL PULL:**
**SPRING & SUMMER**

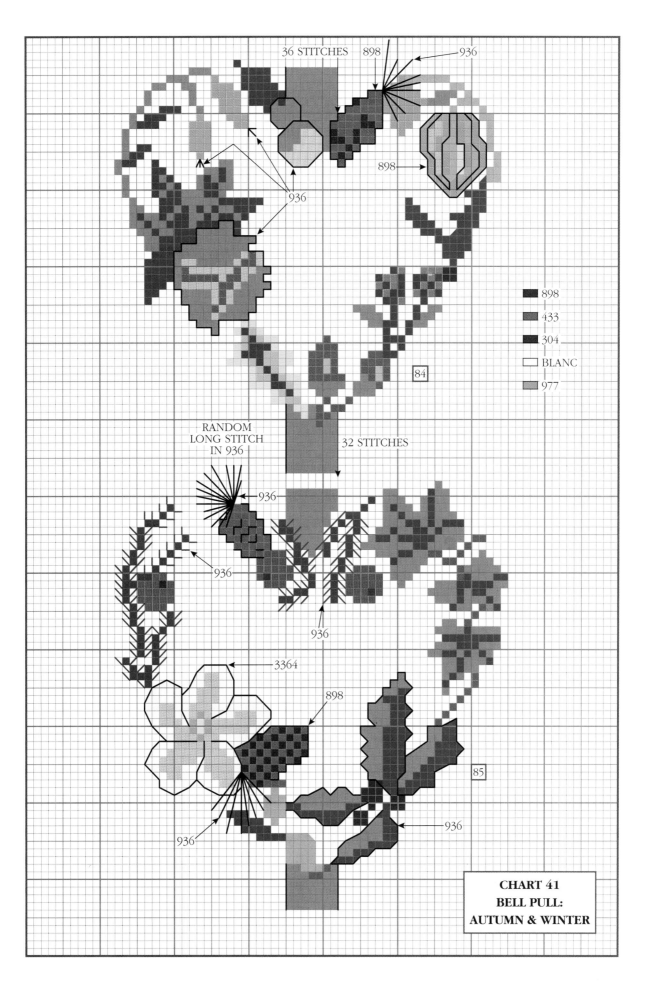

36 STITCHES
898
936
898

936

898

898
433
304
BLANC
977

84

RANDOM
LONG STITCH
IN 936

32 STITCHES

936

936

936

3364

898

85

936

936

**CHART 41**
**BELL PULL:**
**AUTUMN & WINTER**

# 'Rosegarth'

As already mentioned, this design is stitched partly in Designer Silk. To obtain the shaded effect from the silk, work each cross stitch individually rather than in two journeys. To stitch the picture as illustrated, work the house first, stitching towards the pillars at the outer edge. Turn to the rose arch chart and work upwards. Do the same on the other side, joining the arch at the top by stitching the leaves and roses at random.

86

**CHART 42
'ROSEGARTH'**

937
D/S 302
989
D/S 708

CHARTS 42, 43 and 44

| *DMC | ANCHOR |
|------|--------|
| 471 | 0261 |
| 937 | 0263 |
| BLACK | 0403 |
| 3032 | 0392 |
| 738 | 0372 |
| 989 | 0262 |
| 898 | 0381 |
| 317 | 0400 |

3032 →

POSITION
OF WALL

CHART 43
'ROSEGARTH'

317

471
D/S 107
D/S 302
937
D/S 409(LIGHT)

D/S 409(DARK)
BLACK
D/S 705
3032
D/S 708

●● FRENCH KNOTS
IN D/S 302

738
989

898

BEADS

317

POSITION
OF PILLAR

**CHART 44**
**'ROSEGARTH'**

317

898

3032

317

POSITION
OF PILLAR

# Country Cottages

## 'OAKS'

This design is one of a number of pretty cottages as illustrated in the lovely picture on pp94–5. This traditional black-and-white beamed building is a good example of its type, and appropriately named with the surrounding trees and its oak beams both inside and out! 'Oaks' is seen illustrated twice, once in the wooden frame and again as part of the English cottage bell pull.

In both cases the cross stitch was stitched in stranded cottons, using two strands for the cross stitch and one strand for the backstitch outline where appropriate.

### CHART 45

| *DMC | ANCHOR |
|------|--------|
| 898 | 0381 |
| BLACK | 0403 |
| 722 | 323 |
| 436 | 0373 |
| 743 | 0298 |
| WHITE | 01 |
| 3032 | 0392 |
| 936 | 0846 |
| 3347 | 0843 |
| 640 | 0393 |
| 920 | 0339 |

CHART 45
'THE OAKS'

The Oaks

BLACK

BLACK

BLACK

BLACK

898

898

898

| | | |
|---|---|---|
| 898 & 920 | WHITE | 3347 |
| BLACK | 3032 | 640 |
| 898 | 936 | 920 |
| 722 | | |
| 436 | | |
| 743 | | |

86

# 'WILLOWS'

This pretty thatched cottage was based on the mill at Alresford in Hampshire; seen in the morning light, it is most evocative of an Old Master.

## CHART 46

| *DMC | ANCHOR |
|------|--------|
| 562 | 0216 |
| 966 | 0214 |
| 758 | 0337 |
| 792 | 0123 |
| 727 | 0301 |
| 898 | 0381 |
| 739 | 0361 |
| 738 | 0372 |
| 3032 | 0392 |
| 433 | 0357 |

PAGES 94-5
*The English cottage bell pull, 'Oaks',*
*'Willows', 'Old Barn House', 'Rose Cottage',*
*'Crabapple Farm' and 'Moor Farm Cottage'*

CHART 46 'WILLOWS'

3032

3032

792

BACK STITCH
AT RANDOM

FRENCH
KNOT IN
BLUE

433

| 562 | 966 | 758 | 792 | | 727 | 898 | 739 | 433 | | 433 & 898 | 738 | 3032 | 712 | 738 & 739 |

87

Chart with labels: 3032, 936, 88, Crabapple Farm Devon

**CHART 47**
**'CRABAPPLE FARM'**

| ■ 792 | ■ 223 | ■ 632 | ■ 989 | ■ 437 |
| ■ 3685 | ■ 936 | ■ 3032 | □ 738 | |

## 'CRABAPPLE FARM'

'Crabapple Farm' is seen stitched and made up on pp94–5; note that a covered mount is used. The idea of making your own mounts for your pictures is an attractive one; it is both cheap and effective, and adds an original touch to your projects. Basic instructions for the technique are given on p116 (also see Fig 8).

### CHART 47

| *DMC | ANCHOR | PATERNA |
|------|--------|---------|
| 792  | 0123   | 542     |
| 3685 | 0897   | 901     |
| 223  | 0895   | 904     |
| 936  | 0846   | 600     |
| 632  | 0379   | 472     |
| 3032 | 0392   | 463     |
| 989  | 0261   | 604     |
| 738  | 0372   | 444     |
| 437  | 0362   | 445     |

| ■ 304 | ■ 898 | ■ 470 | ■ 936 |
| ■ 937 | ■ 340 | ■ 562 | □ 966 |

# TREES AND GREENERY

The cross stitch on this chart has been worked in two strands of stranded cotton, with the fence and outline on the tree worked in backstitch using one strand only. Tree motif no 92 can be seen in the picture illustrated on pp50–1.

## CHART 48

| *DMC | ANCHOR | PATERNA |
|------|--------|---------|
| 304 | 047 | 950 |
| 937 | 0263 | 610 |
| 898 | 0381 | 430 |
| 340 | 0118 | 343 |
| 470 | 0281 | 693 |
| 562 | 0216 | 662 |
| 936 | 0846 | 600 |
| 966 | 0214 | 614 |

# 'OLD BARN HOUSE' AND 'APPLE COTTAGE'

The following charts show the design for four of the charming cottages stitched on the English cottage bell pull illustrated on p95. They are all sewn on a linen band in stranded cottons, using two strands for the cross stitch and one for the backstitch outline.

'Old Barn House' was based on a barn conversion in Gloucestershire, and 'Apple Cottage' was picked from the apple orchards of Kent!

## CHART 49

| *DMC | ANCHOR | GFT | PATERNA |
|------|--------|------|---------|
| 937 | 0263 | 3902 | 601 |
| 3348 | 0254 | 2000 | 612 |
| 3350 | 0896 | 2088 | 902 |
| 3354 | 074 | 1002 | 905 |
| 301 | 0349 | | 722 |
| 738 | 0372 | 2003 | 444 |
| 414 | 0399 | 1400 | 201 |
| 712 | 0387 | 1000 | 262 |
| 642 | 0392 | 1500 | 463 |
| 938 | 0382 | 1712 | 421 |
| 436 | 0373 | 3302 | 443 |
| 437 | 0362 | | 405 |
| 318 | 0400 | 1450 | 212 |

414

93

Old Barn House ← 937

436

94

414

Apple

Cottages ← 937

937
3348
3350
3354
301 & 738
414
712
642
938
436
437
738
414 & 318
938 & 301

**CHART 49**
**ENGLISH COTTAGES**

# 'MOOR FARM COTTAGE' AND 'ROSE COTTAGE'

'Moor Farm Cottage' is based on a shepherd's home high on the Yorkshire moors, and 'Rose Cottage' nestles amongst the cornfields of Essex. Moor Farm is illustrated twice, once on the bell pull and once in a flower-printed mount. The instructions for making up the covered mounts are included in the techniques on p116 (see also Fig 8).

## CHART 50

| *DMC | ANCHOR | GFT | PATERNA |
|------|--------|------|---------|
| 317  | 0400   | 1450 | 200     |
| 415  | 0398   | 2053 | 203     |
| 932  | 0850   | 1022 | 514     |
| 224  | 0894   | 1002 | 905     |
| 930  | 0851   | 2081 | 512     |
| 936  | 0846   | 3902 | 600     |
| 436  | 0373   | 3302 | 442     |
| 738  | 0372   | 2003 | 444     |
| 3347 | 0843   | 2000 | 613     |
| 3350 | 0896   | 2041 | 901     |
| 223  | 0895   | 3305 | 904     |

317

317 & 415
932
224
930
223
936
3347
WHITE

95

Moor Farm
Cottage

936

96

436
738
3347
224
936
317
3350
223

317

Rose Cottage

936

**CHART 50**
**ENGLISH COTTAGES**

# Pot-Pourri Sachets

The delightful scented sachets pictured overleaf are worked on linen bands, each with a border in a soft, contrasting colour. The bands are made in Germany from pure linen, and the coloured edging is woven into the fabric. The matching tassels are made from the same material as the edging, the perfect compliment to each project.

The designs illustrated are stitched in German flower thread, and each sachet is filled with an appropriately scented pot-pourri. If linen bands are unavailable, strips of any suitable evenweave material could be used.

### CHART 51

| *GFT | ANCHOR | DMC |
|------|--------|-----|
| 1009 | 0216 | 562 |
| 2099 | 0259 | 368 |
| 2041 | 0896 | 3350 |
| 2073 | 041 | 335 |
| 2088 | 042 | 600 |
| 1002 | 075 | 894 |
| 2084 | 0298 | 743 |
| 3522 | 0300 | 727 |
| 3832 | 0210 | 367 |
| 2000 | 0261 | 989 |
| 2035 | 0303 | 742 |
| 1049 | 0304 | 741 |
| 3432 | 098 | 553 |
| 2011 | 0112 | 552 |
| 2068 | 028 | 961 |
| 3215 | 0850 | 931 |
| 3022 | 0403 | BLACK |
| 2079 | 039 | 309 |
| 2061 | 0301 | 744 |

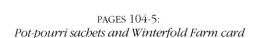

PAGES 104-5:
*Pot-pourri sachets and Winterfold Farm card*

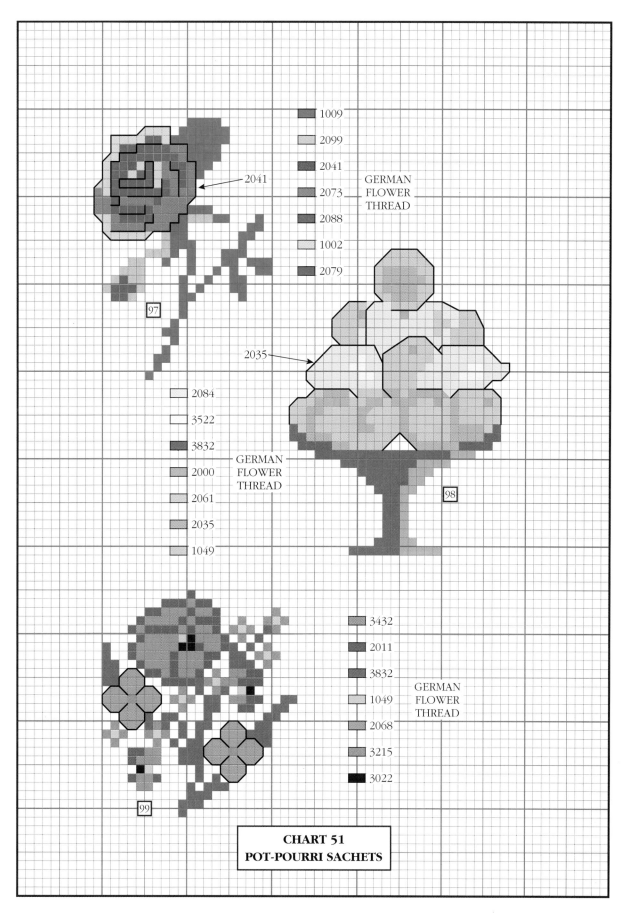

1009
2099
2041
2073
2088
1002
2079

GERMAN
FLOWER
THREAD

2041

97

2035

98

2084
3522
3832
2000
2061
2035
1049

GERMAN
FLOWER
THREAD

3432
2011
3832
1049
2068
3215
3022

GERMAN
FLOWER
THREAD

99

**CHART 51**
**POT-POURRI SACHETS**

# POT-POURRI SACHETS

## CHART 52

| *GFT | ANCHOR | DMC |
|------|--------|-------|
| 3006 | 01 | WHITE |
| 1105 | 046 | 349 |
| 2088 | 042 | 309 |
| 2084 | 0298 | 743 |
| 2082 | 0300 | 744 |
| 2000 | 0261 | 989 |
| 3001 | 0216 | 562 |
| 1005 | 0112 | 552 |
| 3332 | 097 | 554 |
| 1007 | 0393 | 640 |
| 1222 | 0392 | 3032 |
| 3902 | 0263 | 937 |
| 1003 | 0895 | 223 |
| 2023 | 0400 | 317 |
| 3832 | 0210 | 367 |

# MAKING UP

When the cross stitch is complete, check for missed stitches and press the needlework on the wrong side. Place the *wrong* sides together, aligning the edges of the linen band, and pin in position. Slipstitch the two edges together with the matching thread. Turn over a narrow hem at the top of both sections and hem invisibly (see Fig 5).

When the bag is complete, fill with appropriately scented petals and tie with matching flower thread, attaching a tassel at the same time.

*Fig 5 Making scented sachets*

GERMAN
FLOWER
THREAD

☐ 3006    ☐ 2082
■ 1105    ▨ 2000
⊙⊙ 2088   ■ 3001
▨ 2084

3832

100

1005    GERMAN
        FLOWER
3332    THREAD

101

1007
1222
3902
GERMAN    2000
FLOWER    1003
THREAD    3332
2023

2023    102

**CHART 52
POT-POURRI SACHETS**

# La France

The design for the lovely alpine house pictured opposite uses a range of spring colours. It could equally well be stitched in the vibrant colours of summer, possibly using some of the excellent rayon threads available.

Charming thatched houses like 'Normandie' (also pictured) are dotted all over the Normandy hills, with manicured gardens and the most wonderful irises growing in the top of the thatch. Most of the design in chart 54 is planned out for you, but the flower beds in the foreground should be worked at random in either cross stitch or French knots – use the colour key as a guide.

## CHART 53

| *DMC | ANCHOR | PATERNA |
|------|--------|---------|
| 772  | 0259   | 695     |
| 320  | 0261   | 693     |
| 937  | 0263   | 691     |
| 640  | 0393   | 461     |
| 611  | 0832   | 462     |
| 341  | 0117   | 505     |
| 3033 | 0388   | 465     |
| 632  | 0379   | 472     |
| 317  | 0400   | 210     |
| 743  | 0298   | 772     |
| 415  | 0398   | 212     |
| 3032 | 0392   | 463     |

## CHART 54

| *DMC | ANCHOR | PATERNA |
|------|--------|---------|
| 350  | 0334   | 843     |
| 550  | 0102   | 311     |
| 210  | 097    | 313     |
| 758  | 0337   | 874     |
| 937  | 0263   | 601     |
| 794  | 0117   | 562     |
| 435  | 0369   | 403     |
| 640  | 0393   | 462     |
| 738  | 0372   | 444     |
| 744  | 0301   | 714     |
| 3348 | 0261   | 604     |
| 223  | 0895   | 932     |

RIGHT:
*Les Alpes and Normandie*

CHART 53
'LES ALPES'

Les Alpes

640

937

317

| | | | |
|---|---|---|---|
| 772 | 937 | 611 | 3033 |
| 320 | 640 | 341 | 632 |

| | | |
|---|---|---|
| 317 | 415 | BLANC |
| 743 | 3032 | |

CHART 54
'NORMANDIE'

Normandie

# Motifs and Ribbons

## ASSORTED MOTIFS

### CHART 55

| *DMC | ANCHOR | *DMC | ANCHOR |
|------|--------|------|--------|
| 320 | 0261 | 501 | 0878 |
| 433 | 0357 | 436 | 0373 |
| 349 | 046 | 932 | 0850 |
| 304 | 047 | 471 | 0262 |
| 223 | 0895 | 945 | 0311 |
| 3350 | 0896 | 727 | 0295 |
| 898 | 0381 | 722 | 0323 |

**CHART 55**
**ASSORTED MOTIFS**

# RIBBONS

## CHART 56

| *DMC | ANCHOR |
|------|--------|
| 772 | 0259 |
| 936 | 0846 |
| 3364 | 0261 |
| 352 | 09 |
| 350 | 0334 |
| 930 | 0851 |
| 932 | 0850 |

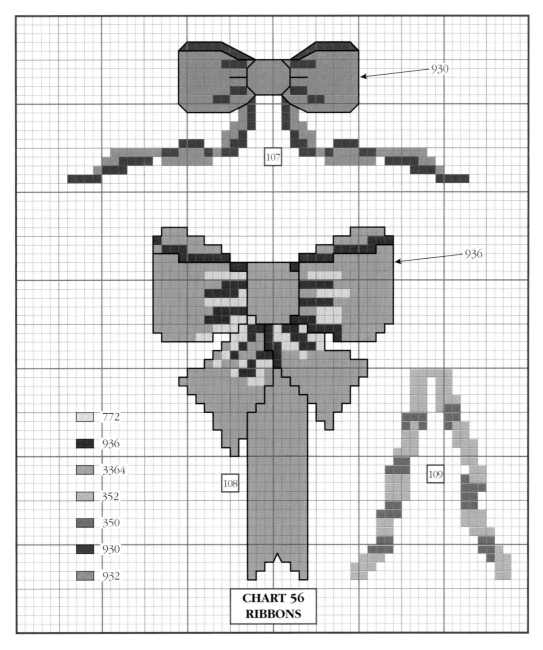

| | |
|---|---|
| 772 | |
| 936 | |
| 3364 | |
| 352 | |
| 350 | |
| 930 | |
| 932 | |

**CHART 56
RIBBONS**

# List of Fabrics

The motifs illustrated in this book are stitched and made up in a number of ways, using a variety of fabrics. The list of materials below indicates which fabric was used for each project as seen in the colour pictures. Feel free to use any evenweave material for your own designs, but always check the stitch and thread count before starting the project.

LINEN: 25 threads to 1in (2.5cm)
Butterfly alphabet
Tree sampler
Bread bag
Wine bag

LINEN: 28 threads to 1in (2.5cm)
Brush and comb set
Black waistcoat
Baskets of fruit, recipe holders
    and picture
Jam pot labels
Country sampler
'Moor Farm Cottage', 'Crabapple
    Farm' and 'Rose Cottage'
Black pepper, and coffee beans bags
Sea salt (unbleached linen)
Christmas rose cushion
Rosebud cushion
Heart rose pincushion
'Oaks'
'Willows'
Basket of fruit clock

LINEN: 30 threads to 1in (2.5cm)
Little alphabet
English village sampler
Four seasons archway pictures
'Rosegarth'
Christmas rose, and bread napkin

AIDA: 14 blocks to 1in (2.5cm)
Basket noteboard in country aida
Tree picture
Message board
French dresser card

AIDA: 18 blocks to 1in (2.5cm)
'Les Alpes'
'Normandie'
Butterfly crystal pot

MURANO: 30 threads to 1in (2.5cm)
Country diary
Recipe folder
Louise door-plate

LINEN BANDS (see suppliers):
Pot-pourri sachets in coloured bands
Cottage and four season bell pulls

MISCELLANEOUS:
Silk holder in Belfast 32 threads
    to 1in (2.5cm)
Footstool in unbleached Belfast 32
    to 1in (2.5cm)
Flower shawl in Afghan fabric
Apple apron in Sanger products
    (see suppliers on p119)
Wooden trinket box in 18 single
    canvas

# Useful Techniques

Detailed instructions for cross stitch are not included in this book, but the techniques needed to make up the projects pictured in the lovely photographs are given below. All the projects are charted and can be mixed and matched to make new designs of your own, the essential requirement being to observe the stitch count and the thread count of the material.

## CARDS

There are many different sorts of blank card available from needlecraft shops, and these are simple to make up into lovely gifts. The finishing techniques for cards will vary, but the following method will suit most brands:

When the stitching is complete, press the design on the wrong side and set aside. Open the folded card completely and check that the design fits in the opening. Apply a thin coat of adhesive (like UHU) to the inside of the opening (see Fig 6). Add the design, carefully checking the position of the stitching, and press down firmly. Fold the spare flap inside and stick in place with either double-sided tape or another thin application of adhesive. Leave to dry before closing.

*Fig 6 Making up a card*

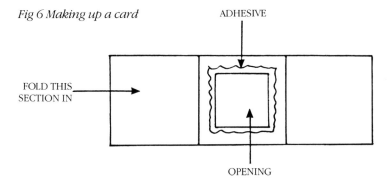

ADHESIVE

FOLD THIS SECTION IN

OPENING

## STRETCHING AND MOUNTING

When mounting small cards or novelty projects the whole procedure can be completed using double-sided sticky tape, but it is worth taking more time and effort on larger projects. You will need either acid-free mounting board, or lightweight foam board, or you can cover a piece of board with a natural fabric like cotton which can be fixed with a rubber-based adhesive and left to dry.

There are three methods of attaching the needlework to the board before framing (see Fig 7):

1 Pin the work to the edge of the board and stick in place with double-sided tape;
2 Pin to a covered board and stitch in position;
3 Pin to the board and lace across the back with strong linen thread.

Whichever method is used, when you pin the material to the board first of all it must be centred, and stretched *evenly* because any wobbles will show when the design is framed! Measure the board across the bottom edge and mark the centre with a pin. Match this to the centre of the bottom edge of the embroidery and, working outwards from the centre, pin through the fabric following a line of threads until all four sides are complete. Then attach it (Fig 7), either by stitching through the needlework to the covered board, or lacing the excess material across the back, or fixing with double-sided tape.

# COVERED MOUNTS

The most simple piece of needlework is given dimension by adding a covered mount to co-ordinate with the design (see Fig 8 p117). If you intend to use an oval or circular-shaped mount you will certainly need to buy it, as to cut these yourself is almost impossible. Square or rectangular mounts can be cut using a craft knife, as the rough edges will be covered by the material.

Press the embroidery on the wrong side and stretch and mount as described above. Cut the mount card the same size as the mounted embroidery and cut an opening the size you require. If the mount has been purchased, check the opening is large enough for the embroidery and set aside.

Referring to Fig 8 for the following method, use the mount as a template, and cut a piece of patterned material at least 1in (2.5cm) wider all the way around. Place the material right side down on a clean flat surface and, using a soft pencil, draw around the inside of the opening. Remove the mount and, using a sharp pair of pointed scissors, cut out the opening about ½in (1.25cm) from the pencil line; clip the edge at intervals. On the wrong side of the mount, apply a thin layer of adhesive to the edge of the opening and add the material, checking the pattern is straight. Stick down and leave to dry. Complete the procedure by pinning and securing the excess material as for stretching and mounting (Fig 7).

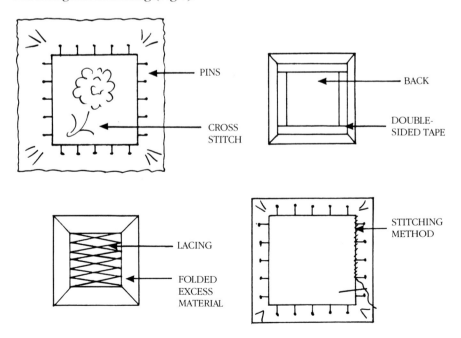

PINS

BACK

CROSS STITCH

DOUBLE-SIDED TAPE

STITCHING METHOD

LACING

FOLDED EXCESS MATERIAL

*Fig 7 Stretching and framing*

*Fig 8 Making covered mounts*

If you intend to make the completed project into a book, you will need to line the inside as well. Cover a piece of this card with the same or co-ordinating material as described above and when dry, slipstitch to the inside (see Fig 8). Ribbons may be added at this point to make hinges or fastenings (see picture on p65).

# MAKING BOOKS

To make up books or folders, there are two methods which can be used: the stitching method, when the book or folder is made in individual sections which are then joined together (see Fig 10) and the scoring method, when the book or folder is made up in one piece (Fig 9). In both cases a softer look can be achieved by covering the card with polyester wadding before making up (see Fig 9).

When the stitching is complete, press on the wrong side and set aside.

# The Scoring Method

Refer to Fig 9 for this method. You will need a piece of stiff card (mount card is ideal) large enough to make the front, back and spine of the book. Lay the card on a clean flat surface and, using a sharp craft knife, score as illustrated; then fold the card, thus forming the spine.

Open the card flat again, lay it on a flat surface and cover it with a slightly larger piece of wadding; sandwich this to the card with the embroidery, checking the position of the stitching – you must also ensure that the original piece of material is large enough to wrap around the card in one section. Pin, using the method described in stretching and mounting; then trim the excess material away, leaving 1in (2.5cm) around the edge, and secure this with strips of double-sided tape. Pressing gently on the scored areas as you do it, fold the front and back up to check that the fabric is secure; then set aside whilst the lin-

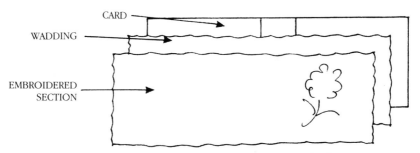

*Fig 9 Making books by the scoring method*

ing is prepared. Cut a piece of co-ordinating material for the lining at least 1in (2.5cm) larger than the completed book; fold the raw edges inside, and slipstitch in position.

# Stitching Method

Referring to Fig 10, you will need three pieces of card, the front, back and spine. To cover them you will need the embroidery, a matching piece of fabric for the back, and a strip for the spine. Cut a piece of lining material and wadding to match each section. The idea is that you make three sandwiches with the lining, card, polyester wadding and the embroidery or back section. To make up one section proceed as follows: lay the lining right side down on a flat surface, and lay the card on top. Add the wadding, and finally the embroidery right side up. Fold in the raw edges, and slipstitch invisibly all the way round.

Complete all three sections in the same way, and finally stitch all three pieces together using matching threads.

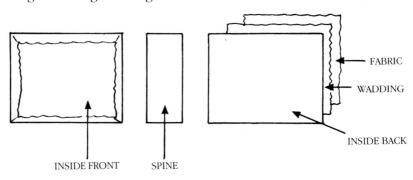

*Fig 10 Making books in three sections*

# Acknowledgements

I would like to thank the following people and organisations for all their help and support that has allowed me to write this, my third cross stitch book: first, my husband, Bill, whose financial management and sales expertise has helped The Inglestone Collection to thrive during a recession!

A very special thank you to Michel Standley, without whom the production at The Inglestone Collection would grind to a halt and who still has time to run her home, bring up a family, stitch and keep me organised!

To the Inglestone team who keep the business running all the year round – Jean, Daphne, Thelma, Rita, Emma, Liz and Diane; also all the staff and trainees at Newholme Day Centre and the Adult Opportunity Centre at Cirencester.

To my dedicated stitchers, without whose addiction this book would not have been possible: Dorothy Presley, Angie Davidson, Hanne Castelo, Di Fallows, Elizabeth Lydan, Vera Greenoff, Carol Lebez, Tamsin O'Brien and Pat Beadle.

To my dear friend Ursula Joka-Deubelius for her hospitality, inspiration and her beautiful German flower thread. Also Rosalind Parnell, whose continued interest in my exploits is as surprising as her fluent German has been invaluable. And all the staff at Vaupel and Heilenbeck, Germany, for their hospitality and their patience with my complete lack of German!

A special thank you to Sara Jane Gillespie, Yew Tree House, Symonds Yat West for sparing the time in her busy schedule to draw the delightful pen and ink sketches which fill this book; to Di Lewis for reading my mind when doing all the lovely photographs; and to Vivienne Wells who continued to have faith in me when others would have given up.

I would also like to thank the following companies for the advice and supplies used in this book: Cara Ackerman from DMC Creative World for generous supplies of fabric and threads; Tunley and Son for framing and art supplies; Framecraft Miniatures Ltd for trinket pots, brush and comb sets, trays and frames; and MacGregor Designs, Burton-on-Trent for wooden pincushions, footstools and trinket boxes. Also Sanger Linen, Switzerland, for the red apron; and Wheatland for the acetate clock.

The beautiful cushions on pp68–9 were made up by Sue Hawkins' excellent finishing service at Needleworks, The Old School House, 67, Hall Road, Cheltenham, Glos GL53 0HP.

Thanks also to the following for needlework supplies: Campden Needlecraft Centre, Chipping Campden, Glos; The Ladies Work Society, Moreton-in-Marsh; Knatty Designs, Stow-on-the-Wold; Tikkit, Gloucester Docks; and Cirencester Needlecrafts. Also Artisan Pinner for printed fabrics and needlecraft supplies.

When writing to any of the suppliers in this book, please include a stamped, addressed envelope for your reply.

# Index

Page numbers in *italic* refer to illustrations